W9-CFW-095

HOUGHTON MIFFLIN
Reading
A Legacy of Literacy

Off to Adventure!

HOUGHTON MIFFLIN   BOSTON · MORRIS PLAINS, NJ

California · Colorado · Georgia · Illinois · New Jersey · Texas

Design, Art Management and Page Production: Kirchoff/Wohlberg, Inc.

ILLUSTRATION CREDITS
4-21 Will Terry. **22-39** Ron Himler. **40-57** Cathy Diefendorf.

Printed in U.S.A.

ISBN: 0-618-03655-5

456789-VH-05 04 03 02 01

Contents

THE LUNCH ROOM

by Rustie Arnott

illustrated by
Will Terry

Strategy Focus

Stan and Carmen want something else
for dessert. What will they get? As you
read, stop now and then to **summarize**
each part of the story.

Stan and Carmen sat in the lunch room.
"Apples again," they both cried. "Yuk!"

"Why can't we have *good* desserts?" asked Stan.

"Yeah, like Ring Rings, and YoHos, and Krispy Kat Bars," said Carmen.

"They'll make your teeth fall out," said the
lunch lady. Her name was LouBelle.

"We never get anything we want," said Stan.

"An apple is a good thing," said LouBelle.

Stan bit into his apple. There was a worm!
Carmen laughed. Milk splashed on the floor.

"Stan-leee! Car-men!" called Lou Belle. "You two get a mop and clean that up."

Stan and Carmen looked into the mop room.
"I don't see a mop," said Carmen.

"Maybe it's in here," said Stan.
He jumped into the bin. Carmen jumped in too.

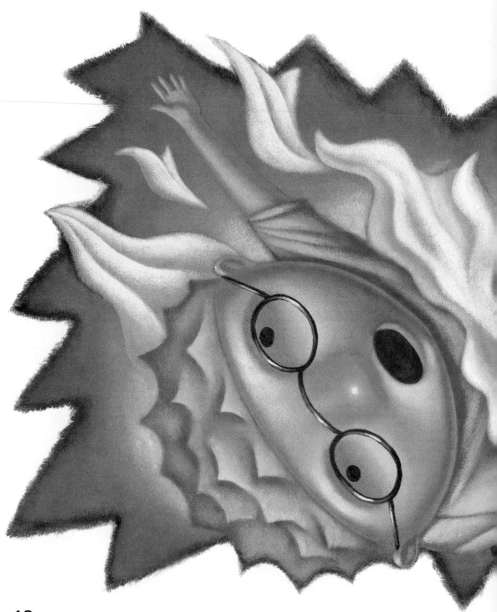

The bin started to spin! It started to fall!
"What's going on?" yelled Stan.

The bin landed with a thud. Carmen and Stan were in the lunch room. But it was much different.

"What'll you have? What'll you have?" said a voice. It was LouBelle! She *really* looked different.

LouBelle gave them cakes and ice cream! They got Ring Rings, YoHos and Krispy Kat Bars!

"Won't our teeth fall out?" asked Carmen.
"Not in *this* lunch room," said LouBelle.

LouBelle kept the sweets coming.
"No more!" cried Stan and Carmen.

They were getting sick! They had to get out!
They jumped in the bin. It started to spin.

Back in the *real* lunch room, Carmen and Stan grabbed two apples. They took giant bites. They were glad to have something good for dessert.

Responding

THiNK ABoUT THE SELECTioN

1 Which part of the school lunches do Carmen and Stan not like?

2 What are three things that happen when Stan and Carmen are in the different lunch room? Tell them in the right order.

WHAT HAPPENS NEXT?

Copy the chart on a piece of paper. Then fill it in for all the events in the story. Be sure to put them in the right order.

Event 1 Stan and Carmen both say "Yuk!" about the apples.
Event 2 They ask LouBelle for sweets for dessert.
Event 3 ?
Event 4 ?

Sacagawea

by Kana Riley

illustrated by Ron Himler

Strategy Focus

How will Sacagawea help Lewis and Clark on their long adventure? **Monitor** how well you understand the events. Reread to **clarify** parts that seem unclear.

Sacagawea (Sack-ah-jah-**wee**-ah) sat in the boat with her baby. She was on a long journey home.

Sacagawea thought about her home. It was the beautiful land of the Shoshone (Show-**show**-nee) people.

24

When Sacagawea was a child, there had been a war.
She had been taken far from her home.

Now Sacagawea was going west with two explorers,
Lewis and Clark.

"Captain Lewis and Captain Clark need our help,"
Sacagawea's husband told her.

Sacagawea helped in many ways. She found meals
of berries and nuts.

In wild waters, Sacagawea saved the explorers'
food and supplies.

Lewis and Clark named a river for Sacagawea. They called it Birdwoman's River.

For weeks, Lewis and Clark raced down rushing
rivers. Like a hawk, Sacagawea watched over them.

One day, Sacagawea knew she was home.
"Shoshone country," she told Lewis and Clark.

At long last, Sacagawea would see her people. She danced with joy.

The Shoshone chief welcomed her. When
Sacagawea saw him, she burst into tears. It was her
brother!

34

Sacagawea spoke for Lewis and Clark. She told her
brother about their great journey.

The chief gave horses to the explorers. He made
sure that the Shoshone treated them well.

Then Lewis and Clark went on with their journey. They still needed Sacagawea's help. She went with them.

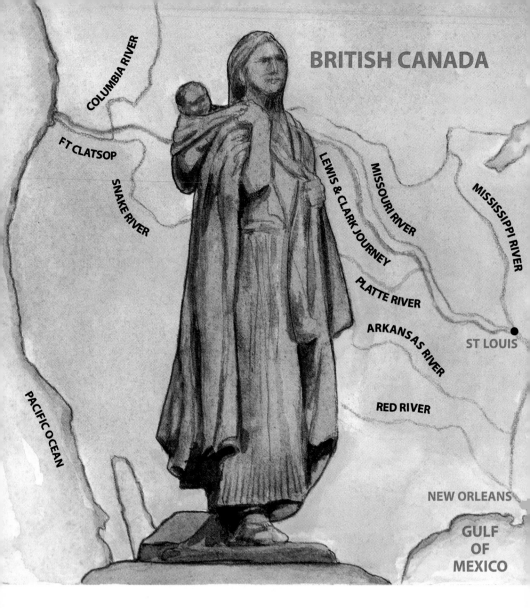

Lewis and Clark went all the way to the Pacific Ocean.
Sacagawea was with them. Together they had
crossed the American West and soared into history.

38

Responding

Think About the Selection

1 Whom does Sacagawea help?

2 Why do you think Sacagawea thought of her home?

Making Inferences

Use a chart to help you make inferences about Sacagawea. Make another chart like this to tell how Sacagawea feels about going home.

Story Clue	What I Know from My Own Life
Sacagawea saves the food and supplies in wild waters.	I know wild waters can be dangerous.

Sacagawea is brave.

Inference

A GREAT DAY FOR SNORKELING

by Nuria Martín

illustrated by Cathy Diefendorf

Strategy Focus

Will Grandma like snorkeling? Read the story carefully and try to **predict** what will happen.

"It's a great day for snorkeling," I said.
"It's a great day for a boat ride," said Grandma.

"Grandma, you'll love snorkeling," I said.
She was afraid to try it. I could tell.

"Snorkeling sounds like something pigs do!" she said. "I'll just stay on the boat and read."

"But you said you'd try!" I told her.
"I guess I changed my mind," she said.

The boat stopped. I pulled on my mask.
"I'm going in without you," I said.

The water looked deep and dark.
But I jumped right in.

The water felt warm as a hug.
I saw colorful fish all around.

Suddenly there was a big splash.
The water got cloudy. I saw only bubbles.

A dark shape was moving closer. My heart pounded fast. Was it a shark?

I popped my head out of the water.
"Grandma!" I shouted back at the boat.

But she wasn't there! I started paddling fast.
Something grabbed my leg!

"Grandma, help!" I yelled again.
"Here I am!" said a voice next to me.

It was Grandma!

"I thought you were a shark," I said.
"That's because I swim like a fish," said
Grandma.

"I thought snorkeling was for pigs!" I said.
"I guess I changed my mind," she said.
We both laughed. Then we dove back under.

Grandma pointed at the blue and yellow fish.
I could tell what she was thinking.
"What a great day for snorkeling!"

Responding

Think About the Selection

1 At the beginning of the story, who says she wants to stay on the boat and read?

2 Why did Grandma jump in the water?

Cause and Effect

Copy the chart on a piece of paper. Then write one cause and one effect to fill in the chart.

Cause	Effect
There was a big splash.	The water got cloudy.
A dark shape was moving closer.	?
?	The girl yelled, "Grandma, help!"

57